My eyes are wet a[...] my views on puri[...] gave me a major [...] shelf, and it's son[...]

ELIZABETH [...]
Student at University of Minnesota—Rochester

I Don't Get You is a beautiful, insightful read. Sherry provides not only relatable and relevant examples but also intriguing insights that opened my eyes to the concept of maintaining healthy relationships with the opposite sex. Whether you are single, dating, married, or wanting to live out purity more intentionally in your everyday life, *I Don't Get You* will give you direction and guidance for pursuing Christlike holiness in your relationships with others.

JEREMY STIMACK
Student at University of Minnesota—Twin Cities

Sherry Graf has put words to the ambiguous, confusing, and invisible cloud of feelings that I have struggled with in my relationships with people of the opposite sex. I needed to recognize my own tendency to emotionally attach in unwarranted situations, and *I Don't Get You* helped me name this internal conflict. I feel encouraged to pursue holiness with my fellow brothers and sisters in Christ in ways that I hadn't considered before reading this book.

STEPHANIE KIPNISS
Student at Vanderbilt University in Tennessee

So often we grow up learning about sexual purity, but we neglect a lifelong pursuit of emotional purity in our conversations and relationships with others. Sherry Graf provides not only a biblical perspective on emotional purity but also a practical method to guard your own and others' hearts in conversation throughout every season of life. This booklet is a must-read for every man or woman looking to sustain healthy, intentional, and God-honoring relationships with people of the same or opposite sex.

JESSICA WEED
Student at University of Colorado—Boulder

I Don't Get You is an incredibly eye-opening resource about how to navigate both relationships and friendships with wisdom. Many people have heard about the importance of setting physical boundaries in relationships, but emotions are frequently left out of the equation. This booklet is a refreshing and practical take on how to guard your heart and honor the people in your life with diligence.

KELLY MORRELL
Student at Lipscomb University in Tennessee

Emotional purity is a topic that I believe is very important for Christians but rarely is discussed. Sherry Graf uses the Bible to support the ideas underlying emotional purity. She has created a book that both men and women can relate to. It is a great resource for small groups and discipleship groups. This book has inspired me to think differently, which will enhance my relationships with others.

SIFA MOSIORI
Rochester Navigators student president at University of Minnesota—Rochester

I plan to share this book with the many college women I mentor and teach. The concept of emotional purity often feels too hard to explain, but Sherry's clear categories of conversation and her description of commitment levels are so helpful. This book has much to apply to my own life as a young married believer and will be important for any and all of my students who are seeking to honor God with their relationships.

MOLLY JENKINS
Mission staff member with The Navigators (Collegiate) at Vanderbilt University in Tennessee

This booklet does a great job of explaining what emotional purity is and how to live it out. I was able to see places I have sometimes unintentionally defrauded my girl friends or myself. And the "yellow flags"—wow! I had been interested in a guy, and those questions made me realize so quickly that we weren't at that level of intimacy. Overall, *I Don't Get You* is a refreshing reminder.

ALY O'CONNOR
Navigators Associate Staff at University of Wisconsin—Whitewater

A GUIDE TO HEALTHY CONVERSATIONS

SHERRY GRAF

NAVPRESS

A NavPress resource published in alliance
with Tyndale House Publishers, Inc.

NavPress is the publishing ministry of The Navigators, an international Christian organization and leader in personal spiritual development. NavPress is committed to helping people grow spiritually and enjoy lives of meaning and hope through personal and group resources that are biblically rooted, culturally relevant, and highly practical.

For more information, visit www.NavPress.com.

I Don't Get You: A Guide to Healthy Conversations
Copyright © 2016 by Sherry Graf. All rights reserved.

A NavPress resource published in alliance with Tyndale House Publishers, Inc.

NAVPRESS and the NAVPRESS logo are registered trademarks of NavPress, The Navigators, Colorado Springs, CO. *TYNDALE* is a registered trademark of Tyndale House Publishers, Inc. Absence of ® in connection with marks of NavPress or other parties does not indicate an absence of registration of those marks.

The Team:
Don Pape, publisher; Caitlyn Carlson, acquiring editor

Cover design by Nicole Grimes

Interior design by Alyssa Force

Cover photograph of note copyright © sumire8/Dollar Photo Club. All rights reserved.

Cover photograph of can telephone taken by Koko Toyama. Copyright © Tyndale House Publishers, Inc. All rights reserved.

All Scripture quotations, unless otherwise indicated, are taken from the Holy Bible, *New International Version,*® *NIV.*® Copyright © 1973, 1978, 1984, 2011 by Biblica, Inc.® Used by permission. All rights reserved worldwide.

Scripture quotations marked NLT are taken from the *Holy Bible,* New Living Translation, copyright © 1996, 2004, 2015 by Tyndale House Foundation. Used by permission of Tyndale House Publishers, Inc., Carol Stream, Illinois 60188. All rights reserved.

Scripture quotations marked KJV are taken from the *Holy Bible,* King James Version.

Some of the anecdotal illustrations in this book are true to life and are included with the permission of the persons involved. All other illustrations are composites of real situations, and any resemblance to people living or dead is coincidental.

Library of Congress Cataloging-in-Publication Data

Names: Graf, Sherry, author.
Title: I don't get you : a guide to healthy conversations / Sherry Graf.
Description: Colorado Springs : NavPress, 2016. | Includes bibliographical references.
Identifiers: LCCN 2016003089| ISBN 9781631465680 (individual) |
    ISBN 9781631464881 (10 pack) | ISBN 9781631465703 (kindle)
Subjects: LCSH: Man-woman relationships—Religious aspects—Christianity. |
    Conversation—Religious aspects—Christianity. | Intimacy (Psychology)—Religious
    aspects—Christianity.
Classification: LCC BT705.8 .G73 2016 | DDC 241/.672—dc23 LC record available
    at http://lccn.loc.gov/2016003089

Printed in the United States of America

22	21	20	19	18	17	16
7	6	5	4	3	2	1

CONTENTS

FOREWORD

Sexual purity is a concept familiar to most people who will read this booklet, and we think we understand what that means in relationships with those of the opposite sex. But in this booklet Sherry Graf has highlighted another term: *emotional purity*. As I read this booklet, I realized that emotional purity, as Sherry describes it, is actually more basic than sexual purity and in fact acts as a gatekeeper to help guard sexual purity.

But emotional purity does more than keep one from immorality. It also guards one's casual—or not-so-casual—conversation with those of the opposite sex. Beyond that, it will help develop healthy relationships between men and women.

Sherry's discussion of 5 Conversation Categories is very helpful. As I read through them, I was reminded of the practice of "due diligence" in the business world. Due diligence is the careful and thorough examination of another company's management, financial condition, future growth prospects, etc., by two companies considering a merger, a buyout, or other organizational and financial contracts.

Sherry's 5 Conversation Categories are in a general sense an outline for relational "due diligence." At the beginning level, these conversational guidelines will help keep casual relationships from becoming awkward or hurtful. Categories 3 through 5 will prove valuable in helping a young man and young woman discern the will of God in leading them into marriage.

This booklet is a valuable contribution to the subject of God-honoring relationships between young men and women. As I read it, I kept thinking, *I want my sixteen-year-old granddaughter to read this.* I trust that it will be widely used.

JERRY BRIDGES
Navigator staff member
Author of *The Pursuit of Holiness*

PART I

The Heart of Healthy Conversations

Jack and Lucy are sitting alone on a moonlit beach. All their other friends have left by this time, and Jack decides to bring the conversation back to where they started earlier as a group, talking about their faith stories. He asks thoughtful questions prompting Lucy to open up more and more. She feels comfortable and at ease with him, so she shares more details about the harder things from her past.

"*I know I mentioned earlier that my parents divorced when I was seven. Ever since then my relationship with my dad has been really rocky. I really miss being close to him."*

Jack leans in, giving her his full attention because he senses that what she is sharing is significant. He shares about his parents' splitting up as well. As an RA on campus, he takes pride in being a good listener. He wants to help Lucy, too.

An hour later, Jack gives her a supportive one-arm hug and a "thanks for sharing" as they part. Lucy leaves, feeling cared for and closer to Jack than to anyone else in her group of friends. Jack leaves, feeling surprised by her vulnerability and a little awkward, but he can't quite figure out why. He also wonders why Emma left the beach so early in the evening. . . . He wishes he had had more time to talk to her.

Can you relate to Jack or Lucy? Many of us have found ourselves in a confusing relationship with someone of the opposite sex. I know I have! When I was in college, I thought I was being such a "good friend" when a guy started pouring out his troubles about his fiancée. I didn't realize my mistake until later . . . when he broke up with her and started pursuing me. A lot of heartache could have been avoided if I had known more about emotional purity.

Christians hear a lot about physical purity, but emotional purity is a vitally important piece of healthy relationships that we tend to miss. In *Sex and the Soul of a Woman*, Paula Rinehart writes, "It is a strange irony that sometimes it is less vulnerable to be sexually involved—to be two strangers in the night—than it is to share your life and your heart with someone."[1] And while both physical and emotional purity are important, all purity really starts with what we do with our hearts, not our hands.

All too often we don't recognize or respect the emotional component happening below the surface of every conversation. And as a result we don't "get" one another. We think we are communicating clearly, but what one person hears is often different from what the other person said. Especially when it comes to talking with the opposite sex.

In her book *The Best Yes*, Lysa TerKeurst says, "Conversational threads are what make up the fabric of relationships."[2] As we build relationships through conversation, invisible emotional ties are being formed. Practicing emotional purity recognizes and respects the potential for those emotional ties. It guards our hearts and the hearts of others as we engage in conversation.

Emotional purity holds our hearts and relationships to a holy standard. It promotes healthy opposite-sex friendships while guarding against defrauding relationships. What do I mean by "defrauding relationships"? Defrauding relationships deceive, seemingly offering something they cannot or will not be able to give. They also rob us of the fulfilling and satisfying relationships that God intends for all His children. Sometimes we defraud without realizing it, as in the situation I faced with that guy in college. He mistook my concern for attachment. (By the way, he later restored the relationship with his fiancée and married her. Whew!) Other times we are aware of our defrauding but like the attention, so we let it continue.

God desires and designed us to have intimate and healthy relationships with Him and each other. By understanding how He designed men and women, especially related to communication, we can find the freedom to enjoy these relationships even more. This booklet lays out simple principles to guard our hearts and protect the hearts of those we relate with. It also teaches how we can have intentional conversations that build appropriate intimacy. As we learn and apply these things, we will grow more into the image of Christ, the Ultimate Lover and Protector of our hearts. When we cultivate healthy relationships with others, we bring honor and glory to God. Friendships that develop and maintain appropriate levels of intimacy are satisfying and a gift from Him. They aren't awkward and don't leave us too emotionally attached, connecting on an emotional level that is inconsistent with where the relationship is in reality. Instead, healthy relationships are fun, freeing, and intentional. Pursuing emotional purity through how we communicate with others will help us in friendships and romantic relationships alike.

Men, if sometimes you don't understand women, keep reading! This emotional purity stuff might sound like it's touchy-feely and not for you. Don't be fooled. Men also form emotional bonds and need to practice emotional purity in how they connect with and communicate with women. Doing so will help you honor the women you interact with. Trust me, women will really appreciate it if they know they can rely on you to not mess with their hearts. Emotional purity can help you keep female friends you don't have any feelings for from attaching to you in a way that goes beyond friendship. In other words, it can keep that conversation from getting awkward. It will also help guide you as you lead one special woman into a deep, rewarding relationship.

A young man from our ministry years ago heard these principles early on in his dating relationship with his girlfriend. He had at least two years left in college, and the guidelines in this booklet helped him pace their relationship. He intentionally didn't go too emotionally deep too soon with her because he knew he didn't want to get married until after graduation. As time progressed he guided their hearts into deeper attachment until he was ready to commit to her for life.

Practicing emotional purity now as a single person helps you form healthy relating habits that you will carry into all future relationships—whether you remain single or get married. We will talk later about what emotional purity looks like after marriage and how it can help you go deeper with your spouse while safeguarding your marriage from outside attachments.

Stop and Discuss

1. Reread the story at the beginning of this section. Why did Lucy feel so close to Jack after their talk? Was that feeling mutual? Why or why not?

2. Why was this conversation significant to Lucy?

3. Did Jack realize how important this conversation was to Lucy? Why or why not?

4. Have you ever found yourself in Jack's situation when a conversation with someone became awkward? Describe what happened. When and how did the conversation turn from lighthearted to deep?

5. Have you ever found yourself in Lucy's situation, where you became more attached to a friend after a deep conversation? Why do you think you felt that way?

6. Do you think Jack and Lucy had ever heard of emotional purity? Why or why not?

7. How much time have you spent thinking about emotional purity? What role has it played in your life up to this

point? Looking back, do you recognize the emotional component in conversations with the opposite sex (e.g., invisible emotional ties being formed)? Describe any conversations that come to mind.

Guard Your Heart

I remember reading a snarky and slightly bitter blog post about guarding your heart. The writer felt that emotional purity was unbiblical and had kept her from getting to know men she later wished she had gone deeper with. I don't know her or all of her story, but I think she was misinformed about what emotional purity really is and why guarding her heart is important. The Bible actually has a lot to say on this subject.

God created us for relationship. These relationships originate in our hearts as we attach emotionally to one another. Our hearts, relationships, and lives belong to Him. The Bible mentions *heart* and *hearts* over eight hundred times, referring not only to our physical hearts but to the seat of our lives and emotions. God's greatest commandment to us is to love Him with all our hearts, and the second is to love our neighbors well (Matthew 22:37-39).

Proverbs 4:23 says, "Above all else, guard your heart, for everything you do flows from it." These words are from a father to his son as he implores him to guard his heart because it is the source of inner life. The New Living Translation says, "It determines the course of your life." And the King James Version translates this verse as, "Keep thy heart with all diligence, for out of it are the issues of life." Guarding our hearts is important because our hearts affect all areas of our lives. From our hearts come all our thinking, decisions, feelings, actions, and motives.

Our hearts haven't changed since biblical times. We still need to guard our hearts, and the hearts of others, in order to love God and our neighbors well. A firm and growing relationship with Christ is the first step toward protecting our hearts and developing fulfilling relationships. Christ fills our "emotional tanks" and defends against unhealthy attachments. We can then look to others to bless them, not simply to meet our own needs; we can love them better.

If I could talk to the woman who wrote the bitter blog post about guarding her heart, I would ask her to reconsider her definition. Guarding our hearts isn't about putting walls up to keep others out. It is about respecting our hearts and the hearts of others. It actually frees us up to go deeper with the people we are really committed to and who are committed to us. The part of us that God designed to "determine the course" of our lives is worthy of great care and respect.

Stop and Discuss

1. Why do you think Proverbs 4:23 is important?

2. What do you think of when you read this verse? What does "guarding your heart" look like to you?

3. How have you seen your heart affect your attitudes, actions, and life?

4. Have you responded negatively to the idea of emotional purity in the past, or encountered someone else with a negative view? How could learning what the Bible says about our hearts impact a negative perspective of emotional purity?

What Makes a Conversation Intimate?

I'm *not* saying you should never have a conversation with the opposite sex in order to guard your heart and theirs. Please, please, please don't hear that! If you are single, there's nothing wrong with talking to people and keeping your radar out for a potential deeper relationship. In fact, it's healthy to develop friendships with people of both the same and the opposite gender. But there are ways to do this while practicing emotional purity. The key is to understand what really makes a conversation intimate. God designed our hearts to attach to others through conversation. The more intimate the discussion, the greater the emotional bond we form.

Two things (among others) make a conversation intimate: (1) context and (2) content. Understanding these two things will help us practice emotional purity.

As a reminder, emotional purity promotes healthy intimacy while guarding against unintended or unhealthy attachment. For an example of unintended attachment, and how context plays into it, let's go back to Jack and Lucy that night on the beach.

> *"You're such a good listener and a great friend,"*
> *Lucy whispers as Jack hugs her good-bye. Her*
> *heart suddenly feels full of affection for him. She*
> *is a little surprised by this but also enjoys it.*
>
> *Jack shrugs off the compliment, feeling a bit*
> *awkward. "It's no big deal."*
>
> *Lucy smiles up at him. "No, really, you*
> *would make a great pastor someday."*

Jack feels like he was being a good Christian brother by listening to Lucy. "Thanks!" he says. *But he walks away thinking,* I just wish Emma could see that side of me. *Later as he lies in bed, he thinks,* Lucy seems like a good friend already. Maybe I'll ask her for help in getting to know Emma better.

Jack and Lucy did what is normal and natural—developing a friendship. The night began innocently and safely—in a large group of people sharing some of their faith stories together. But when the *context* changed to one-on-one, the potential for emotional intimacy changed as well. This would be great if Jack and Lucy were intentionally pursuing a romantic relationship, but they weren't. Unfortunately, they were both unaware of the invisible emotional bonds forming. Context is key in how much our hearts attach in conversation.

Remember the guy friend that I unintentionally split up from his fiancée in college? The problem was not only that we were discussing this one-on-one—what we were discussing was also a big issue.

He didn't just share about his relationship troubles; he was a very emotional guy and shared a lot of his feelings as well.

When we move from sharing what we think to how we feel, our hearts are more prone to form emotional ties. That is why the second factor of intimacy in conversation is *content*—what we share. In other words, what we talk about directly correlates with our level of intimacy with another person.

God created our hearts to attach when the context and content are intimate. It does matter, though, who is doing the sharing. I think this happens in general more for women because we tend to share our feelings more. But it can happen for men, too. A deep conversation doesn't always equal a deep attachment on both ends. And the "listener" is often unaware of the attachment forming on the other end. So you can see now that not only does the context matter, but what we share is just as important for developing intimacy—or avoiding it when it is unhealthy or unwanted.

Okay, so now we know that God created us for relationship, that these relationships form through conversation, and that the context and content of those conversations determine how emotionally attached we become. Knowing this, how do we know when what we share is okay or too much?

PART II

How to Have Healthy Conversations

Five Conversation Categories

As Christians, we want to enjoy God-honoring friendships. But how do we keep relationships with the opposite sex platonic when friendship is all that is desired? And for the special someone who catches your eye, what is okay to talk about with her or him? How can you get to know one another without getting prematurely attached? Being aware of the context and content helps, but breaking it down to basic building blocks of conversation gives us a better grasp of where a conversation is going emotionally. The 5 Conversation Categories help us do just that.

The following 5 Conversation Categories[1] help raise awareness of the emotional level beneath every interaction. As we navigate each category, we can intentionally develop deeper intimacy with our boyfriend, girlfriend, or spouse. Understanding the categories can help us recognize when the discussion slips too deep with a platonic friend so we can move it back to a healthy, honoring level of friendship. Each category can be intimate depending on how deeply we share. As we progress from 1 to 5, the categories lend themselves to increasing emotional intimacy.

CATEGORY 1: BIO-DATA

This is where relationships usually start and where connections begin. Bio-data involves the facts about a person. You discover that you both like to ski, play Settlers of Catan, drink coffee, or read, or that you both grew up in Tuscaloosa or like a certain band. The questions are endless: Do you have siblings? What is your favorite flavor of ice cream? Do you like the Packers or the Vikings? Did you ever have a pet hamster? Where did your family take summer vacations? What church do you go to? Would you rather read a book or take a hike? Do you prefer spicy tacos or fried chicken? Paper Bible or electronic? It takes a lifetime to cover all the get-to-know-you questions. My husband, Jeff, and I recently celebrated our fifteenth wedding anniversary, and I am still learning new things about him. I love that God made us so complex; it is fun that after so much time I still have new territory to uncover!

CATEGORY 2: TESTIMONY, FAITH STORY, OR SPIRITUAL JOURNEY

It is really fun to hear how others have come to understand God's amazing love for them. I love hearing other people's faith stories. But it can also lend itself to deeper, more emotional content. So one word of caution when sharing alone with someone of the opposite sex: stick with basic facts at first. Depending on how openly you share your testimony, you might venture into categories 3, 4, or 5, which lend themselves to deeper intimacy. There is plenty of time to share more if or when the relationship progresses. It is always safer to share in a group, where you will be less likely to share "too much."

For example, remember how Lucy shared with her group of friends that her parents divorced? But later when she was alone with Jack, she opened up about some of her daddy-wounds surrounding that divorce—she jumped to the most intimate category in one sentence. That conversation went much deeper very quickly.

Some questions to ask include the following: When and how did you become a Christian? Why did you choose Christianity? Did you grow up in a Christian home? When and how did this decision to follow Christ start making a real difference in your life?

CATEGORY 3: DREAMS

I'm not talking about that funky dream I had last night where I loaded a dishwasher full of popcorn. What I mean by "dreams" is what keeps you excited and awake thinking about it at night. This topic tends to be more bonding because of what dreams reveal about a person—the whys. People's motivations drive their dreams. When you know their motives, you know what makes them tick. Why they go after what they go after. Why they say yes or no to life's opportunities.

When Jeff and I were dating, he switched his major from mechanical to civil engineering. We dreamed that we might live overseas someday, and knowing how to help people get clean water seemed a better fit. (Plus he realized he didn't like sitting at a desk all day!) So knowing part of Jeff's dream helped me understand why he decided to switch majors.

Here are a few examples of questions that fall into this category: What do you dream about doing someday? What is on your "bucket list," and why? When you were five years old, what did you want to be when you grew up? Do you still want to pursue that? Why or why not?

CATEGORY 4: FEARS

I don't mean your real and understandable fear of spiders. I had to bravely kill an enormous one yesterday when my husband was not home. What I mean here is deeper heart-level fears. For example: What scares you the most? Getting married? Never getting married? Having kids? Not having kids? Your child dying? Cancer? Finding a job after college? Not succeeding in your career? What keeps you awake at night worrying? Why? When did that fear first develop? How do you handle your fears? Are they paralyzing you? Does your spiritual life help you with your fears? How? Emotional ties are more easily formed when we share fears because emotion is attached to them. And when you share that you are afraid of having kids because you had such a terrible childhood, you are quickly going from just the facts to deeper feelings (and hurts) of why (content).

CATEGORY 5: DEEPEST HURTS

We live in a broken world. Other people sin, and it hurts us. We sin and hurt others. We all have wounds that cut to the core of our being. And our deepest wounds often define some of the inmost places of our hearts. Just like our dreams, wounds motivate and influence our actions, thoughts, and choices. Understanding someone else's (and your own) deepest hurts gives you knowledge not just about who they are but why they are who they are.

Revealing the hard things from your life with

someone bonds you to them. This can be very healing and enriching in a marriage or with another brother or sister in Christ you have a close friendship with. Share details about your wounds only with the people you trust the most, those who are most committed to you. Personally, I didn't share a single deepest hurt with my husband until after we were engaged. And then I probably shared only one! I wanted to know he was fully committed to me before I opened up this deep part of my heart to him.

Some questions fall into this category: What do you most regret? What are the biggest wounds from your past? Who in your past has hurt you the most? Why? What happened? Have you ever had counseling for that wound? How has God brought healing to these areas? Is there anyone from your past who hurt you that you still need to forgive? Are you carrying a grudge or bitterness against anyone?

*   *   *

So what is okay to say when? We all have to prayerfully decide for ourselves. Err on the side of saving your heart. In general, a woman's heart can attach more quickly than a man's because women tend to be more verbal and in tune with their feelings. Either way, we want to be protecting each other as we converse. Even if it feels good to open up, it might not be the right time.

Consider this guideline for all of your interactions:

The level of intimacy should always equal the level of commitment.

Remember the couple I shared about in the beginning who dated throughout college? In the early stages of their relationship the young man intentionally avoided deeper topics, knowing they would lead to attachment before he was ready to commit. In the same way, a man and woman who have just met will avoid sharing intimate details about themselves and will instead focus on learning facts about each other. An engaged couple will likely share facts and feelings from Category 4 and 5. It is safer for them to attach emotionally because of their commitment to stay together.

Remember, context and how deeply you share are important. You can share facts from Category 5 (deepest hurts) in front of a large group without forming attachments to anyone there. When alone with a woman or man who is not your girlfriend or boyfriend, it is safest to stick with the facts and not venture into the deeper categories.

Stop and Discuss

1. To what extent is Christ your main source of fulfillment? Are you looking to others more than to God to meet your emotional needs? Explain.

2. What do you think of the 5 Conversation Categories? How can they help you love others well (either in avoiding uncommitted intimacy *or* in pushing yourself to go deeper when appropriate)?

3. What categories would you add or take out, if any? Why?

4. How deeply do you think you should share with someone you aren't in a committed relationship with? Why?

5. Is there anyone in your life whom you think you have unintentionally encouraged to emotionally attach to you? How do you know?

6. If you are in a serious relationship, are you both in agreement with how much you should share with someone else of the opposite sex?

What If You've Already Shared Too Much?

Jack and Lucy continue to spend a lot of time together. Lucy knows by now that they will never date but still holds on to the friendship. All of their friends assume they are dating because they are so close. Jack and Lucy deny this, claiming they are truly platonic. They don't see anything wrong with their friendship. A month later, Jack starts pursuing Emma. Lucy is surprised by how much it hurts to have him spending so much time with someone else. And Emma doesn't like that he is "best friends" with another girl.

What do we do if we realize we have already formed emotional ties with someone who is not committed to us? I get this question every time my husband and I share these principles with a group. You aren't alone, and there is hope for healing. We have all overshared at some point. We can ask Christ to take control of that friendship and help us make healthy choices from here on out. Pray what King David prayed to

God: "Create in me a pure heart, O God, and renew a steadfast spirit within me" (Psalm 51:10). Talk with a trusted mentor and ask for specific counsel. Pray with a mentor to break any soul ties (invisible spiritual bonds) that may have formed.

Consider that it might be necessary to stop seeing that person as often, or even at all, for a while. Sometimes it is too painful and confusing to maintain the friendship at the same level. Hopefully, the friendship can be spared with time, but we should give our hearts space and time to heal.

If you think that one of your friends might be emotionally attached to you, and you have no intention of dating him or her, you might need to clarify your relationship. Honor your friend by telling him or her what you have learned about emotional purity; don't completely pull away and drop out of the friendship. Instead, use the 5 Conversation Categories to guide your interactions with your friend in the future. Keep the level of intimacy equal with your commitment. If you currently spend a lot of time alone together, be intentional about hanging out in groups instead.

Six Ways We Unintentionally Defraud One Another Emotionally

de·fraud: *to deprive of something by deception or fraud.*[2]

1. **Men defraud women** or lead them on. Women perceive communication differently. When a man carries on deep conversations alone with a woman with no intention of romance, he is defrauding her heart. He deceives her into thinking he is interested in a romantic relationship. He takes her heart without any commitment to protect it. Men can also abuse this knowledge and use her heart to get to her body.

2. **Men defraud men** when they give the message that they are good friends but never share who they really are inside— their fears, dreams, or deepest hurts— with each other.

3. **Men defraud themselves** when they deprive themselves of the opportunity to experience rich community by never going deep with one another. They only ever talk about sports and events, even in contexts where it would be helpful to share more deeply, as in a men's group or Bible study.

4. **Women defraud men.** A man might think a woman is really interested in him if she pays him special attention. She enjoys spending a lot of time with him, baking him cookies, and writing him notes, but she isn't attracted to him romantically. She is defrauding him into thinking there might be something more.

5. **Women defraud one another.** When a friend comes home after having coffee with a guy, and her roommate reads into every little thing he said or did, the roommate is defrauding her. Forcing her to imagine, interpret, or dwell on the details of her evening does not help her

guard her heart. It deprives her of the freedom to enjoy the friendship for what it is. Instead, the roommate can help by keeping their conversation based in reality.

6. **Women defraud themselves.** When a woman lets her mind wander off, dreaming of a future with a guy who just asked her to dinner, she is defrauding herself. She deprives herself of fully enjoying that friendship at its current level and deceives herself into thinking it is something more than it is. Asking God to help her stop mentally rushing ahead will free her up to enjoy the friendship.

PART III

Dependency

Have you ever had a friendship with someone of the same gender that was a little too emotionally draining? I have—it can really put a strain on your friendship. Practicing emotional purity is important in relationships with people of the same sex, too.

We all want to be known. This is natural and how God created us as relational beings. But sometimes we look to others—even friends of the same sex—too much to fill our emotional needs. If we look to others to listen to all our problems, be our constant companions, or continually lift us up, we are probably forming an unhealthy attachment to them. Being this needy will scare off anyone who isn't doing the same thing to us.

We all must start by turning to Christ for our heart needs. If you don't know how to do this, try finding a mature Christian to mentor you. Then, with the 5 Conversation Categories in mind, intentionally do *not* go too deep in conversation, even with a friend of the same sex. Wait until you are in a healthy relationship with Christ, being filled up emotionally from Him. With your "emotional tank" full from the One who loves you the most, you will be able to more sincerely pour out on others. This doesn't mean we don't receive love from others; they simply are no longer our primary source.

If you struggle with becoming too emotionally dependent, try seeking out relationships with several friends so you do not become overly dependent on one person. Practicing emotional purity is vital to developing healthy friendships.

Same-Sex Attraction

Several months ago I attended a seminar on helping others with same-sex attraction. I was struck by what I heard: that for women (and perhaps for men as well), unhealthy emotional dependency is often the gateway into same-sex attraction. By guarding against unhealthy emotional attachments, someone with same-sex attraction can avoid the temptation to act on these emotions. So the guidelines laid out in this booklet still apply! If you are attracted to someone of the same sex, it would be wise to keep the conversations light and avoid talking too deeply about feelings.

This booklet isn't designed to comprehensively address this difficult situation. It is important for anyone dealing with same-sex attraction to share about that attraction with a trusted Christian mentor or counselor who can help them develop healthy boundaries and satisfying friendships. The following resources can also offer help and insight if this is something you are facing.

Resources for Further Study:

Emotional Dependency by Lori Rentzel
The Heart of Female Same-Sex Attraction by
    Janelle Hallman
People to Be Loved by Preston Sprinkle

Homosexuality and the Christian by Mark A.
    Yarhouse
Is God Anti-gay? by Sam Allberry
Washed and Waiting by Wesley Hill

PART IV

Emotional Purity and Dating

As time passes, Jack spends more and more time with Emma. He hopes that by the end of the summer they will be in a committed relationship. But Jack has learned a few things about a woman's heart along the way. After a couple of awkward and painful conversations with Lucy, he realizes he needs to be more careful to not get so close in a platonic friendship. His attachment to Lucy is more like that of a brother, but he knows it hurts her now that he is spending more time with Emma and less time with her. He feels bad about hurting her and misses her too, but he can't spend as much time with her as before and

still have time to pursue Emma. He is excited to get to know Emma better, and he also wants to protect both their hearts from getting too close too soon. How can he do this?

Before You Start to Date

Recently a young friend of mine shared with me about a guy she was interested in. She wanted to know my opinion, so I went through a few of what I consider my "yellow-flag" questions. Yellow-flag questions simply help us slow down and consider before diving too deeply into a relationship. Our answers may indicate a need to slow down and proceed with caution in any relationship. It is a good idea to answer these questions before becoming attached to someone.

Christian fellowship groups on campus or small groups at church are great places to get to know a potential boyfriend or girlfriend. Get around this person of interest in a group setting, and try to get any yellow flags answered early on in the relationship or before dating. (These questions are relevant in dating relationships where marriage is the end goal.)

You might not know the answers yet, and that is okay. The person you're interested in might not know the answers either. But the answers are things that will make a big impact on your future lifestyle and are worth thinking about.

Some possible questions are:

1. Is this person pursuing Christ? (This is really more of a *red* flag—if someone isn't a committed Christian and you are, it is unbiblical and unwise for you to date him or her.) How do you know?

2. How do they treat you and their family members? (When I was dating my husband, I was impressed by how respectfully he talked about his mom and his sister. I knew this was a good indication of how he would treat me.)

3. Does this person want to live in the United States or overseas? In a big city or out in the country?

4. Does this person want to go into vocational ministry or serve God in the workplace?

5. Does this person want to be a parent someday? If so, does he or she want a small or big family? Does he or she want to have one parent stay home and raise the kids? Which one? Or does he or she think both parents should work outside the home?

If you're in a relationship where these questions seem too serious, that's a good sign that the relationship *isn't* serious and you should be cautious of too much intimacy.

When You Start to Date

Dating is fun and exciting. Enjoying a budding romance is a beautiful example of how God designed us to connect intimately with Him and others. The 5 Conversation Categories help us skillfully and intentionally develop a relationship. Don't be afraid to open up to each other; do it intentionally and honestly. Maintain a level of intimacy that matches the level of commitment. As the commitment grows, so can the conversational intimacy. Most importantly, surrender the relationship to God for Him to guide. He often does this through the wise counsel of a trusted mentor.

Some of us might be afraid to share our hearts because of past broken relationships. This was true for me when I started dating my husband. I was "gun-shy" from a past breakup that had been very close to engagement. I had to force myself to prayerfully open my heart to Jeff as I felt God leading me. If this is true for you, too, ask God to heal those hurts and speak truth to any lies you might believe from that experience (e.g., "no woman is trustworthy" or "all men are jerks").

In order to move forward, we also have to surrender our hearts to God. By acknowledging that our hearts belong to Him, to guard or give away as He sees fit, we will start to trust Him and this other person. This doesn't guarantee we won't get hurt again. Unfortunately, there are no earthly relationships without some level of risk. But it is an important step toward finding freedom and moving forward.

Emotional Purity and Physical Purity Are Connected

As a single person, I had no idea how much my sexuality and emotions were connected. I wish I had known then! As a married woman, I've noticed a direct correlation between my emotional closeness to my husband and my desire for physical connection. This is because God intentionally created women to have the two intertwined. Emotions are tied up with their sexuality. The more a woman shares her heart with a man, the more she wants to share the rest of herself as well. In *Sex and the Soul of a Woman*, Paula Rinehart shares, "Vulnerability of the heart is always supposed to precede, by a long shot, vulnerability of the body, which is another euphemism for sex."[1] This emotional and physical vulnerability is a beautiful thing within the protective boundaries of marriage. So whether you are single or married, practicing emotional purity is key to practicing physical purity. Men can use this knowledge about women to help protect purity both physically and emotionally. I'm using generalizations here because I think women's emotional purity affects their physical purity more than it does for men. However, there are certainly exceptions to this, and men should also be on alert—especially if they are struggling with physical purity in a relationship.

Somebody once said that the more we undress emotionally, the easier it is to undress physically. By intentionally not going too deep too fast emotionally, we can avoid the temptation to go too far physically before marriage.

Stop and Discuss

1. Write down your own possible yellow-flag questions. Discuss what you wrote and why.

2. How will you apply the information you have learned so far to your dating relationships (current or future)?

3. Is the idea of emotional and physical purity being connected new to you? What do you think about it?

PART V

Emotional Purity and Marriage

Emotional purity is just as important for your future marriage (should you marry) as it is when you are single. The healthy habits of relating that you practice as a single person will help you develop intimacy in and protect your marriage. If my husband and I only ever talked about our kids' soccer and swim schedules but never shared our feelings, we would not have a very close relationship. So we intentionally and regularly check in with how we are really doing. Often, we end the evening asking, "What was the best part of your day and why?" And we occasionally take the time to dream together about the future. This is emotionally bonding and fun, and it adds intimacy to our marriage. Paula Rinehart says, "Real vulnerability followed by genuine commitment to a person make sexual intimacy one of the best joys on earth. This sort of joy is simply not possible in a relationship that is not for keeps."[1] So by intentionally going deeper emotionally in marriage, we are improving our love life in other areas as well.

Practicing emotional purity also helps protect marriages from outside emotional attachments that could lead to physical affairs. We might think that we would never be tempted, but the American Association for Marriage and Family Therapy states, "A new crisis of infidelity is emerging in which people who never intended to be unfaithful are unwittingly crossing the line from platonic friendships into romantic relationships."[2] A national poll showed that "15 percent of married women and 25 percent of married men have had sexual affairs . . . [and] an *additional* 20 percent of married couples have been impacted by emotional infidelity."[3]

To protect our hearts and marriages from unintended emotional affairs, we need to make sure our spouses are our best friends. Maintaining the right context and level of intimacy while in conversation with people of the opposite gender will guard against an emotional affair. We should always keep our spouses as our closest confidants. Paul E. Miller in *A Loving Life* describes his marital guidelines like this:

> *My relationship with my wife is like a wonderful garden with a solitary 'no': I cannot touch or develop emotional intimacy with another woman. That 'no' narrows and limits my life. It provides a frame for my love to Jill. I am keenly aware that I can destroy a forty-year marriage in five minutes. That limiting, instead of boxing us in, lets the story come alive.*[4]

All too often, affairs start off innocently, with a lonely spouse sharing too openly with a "caring friend," Facebook friend, online chat buddy, or coworker. Too many people are caught off guard when what seems like a selfless act of "being a good friend and listener" turns quickly into physical intimacy. If we share intimate details with someone other than our spouses, the potential for physical intimacy is soon to follow. We need to be cautious and remove ourselves from the situation before something we never intended happens.

Interacting in groups at work is a good idea, especially on projects that take up a lot of time. If a conversation turns to feelings more than facts, change the subject or walk away. Sometimes even too many compliments and positive feedback on the job can foster emotional attachments. This is especially true when someone isn't feeling valued by his or her spouse at the time.

A good friend of mine blindly fell into an emotional affair. Two years into her marriage she started writing to an ex-boyfriend with the intention of sharing her newfound faith in Christ. Her marriage was rocky at the time, and this reconnection with an old flame quickly grew into an emotional affair. Eventually she realized that even though nothing physical had happened with this other man, her emotional attachment was wrong. She ended the correspondence and confessed to her husband. He forgave her, and through counseling they were able to restore their marriage. In order to protect her heart and marriage from another affair, they set up some safeguards.

Anyone can easily find himself or herself in a conversation that borders on sharing something too emotionally bonding. To guard our own marriage, my husband and I share with each other if we have had an emotional conversation with someone of the opposite sex. That brings both of us into the "circle" of conversation and keeps it emotionally neutral. We still enjoy meaningful relationships with other couples where, all together, we share more deeply with one another.

As a single, you can protect your own heart and help protect the marriages around you by practicing emotional purity in your conversations. If you are married, discuss with your spouse what boundaries you want in place with opposite-sex friendships. Agree together how best to protect your marriage while enjoying outside friendships.

PART VI

Pursuing Emotional Purity Together

*After spending the summer getting to know
each other, Jack and Emma are dating. He
is intentionally pursuing her heart as his
commitment to her increases. Emma feels
cherished and safe with Jack. He no longer spends
a lot of time alone with Lucy. Lucy has learned the
hard way how to guard her heart around men.
She is fun and lighthearted in her interactions
with her brothers in Christ. And when Ted started
showing special attention to her, she was cautious
but optimistic. She intentionally avoided spending
a lot of time alone with him, choosing to get to*

know him in a group. Since he learned about the 5 Conversation Categories, he is following that guideline as he pursues her heart. He knows to keep the level of intimacy in their conversations equal with how ready they are to commit to each other.

I sincerely hope you have a clearer understanding of how to intentionally guard someone's heart and your own. When you recognize the emotional ties that form through conversation, you are able to better lead others into healthy conversations. When you find yourself talking alone with someone of the opposite sex, stick with the facts. Wait until you are committed to each other to share more deeply. Remember, the level of intimacy should equal the level of commitment.

If you marry, the 5 Conversation Categories can help you continue to pursue your spouse's heart. The categories can also act as a guide as you relate to other men and women in your life, such as your brothers and sisters in Bible study. When the relationships are ready, try to go beyond just the facts. Share what is really going on in your heart so you can be encouraged and supported. I cherish it when other women trust me enough to go beyond surface issues. If you struggle with opening up with your friends, the 5 Conversation Categories can be a good challenge to go deeper.

A long time ago I shared these principles with a car full of student friends. Several weeks later one of the women in the group told me she didn't think the Conversations Categories would really work. But she had decided on her own to give it a go. As time passed, she realized that she was enjoying her friendships with guys a lot more than before. She no longer struggled with wondering whether there was something more than just a friendship. Practicing emotional purity freed her up to have satisfying opposite-sex friendships! I was excited for her, and I hope that you find that the same thing happens for you.

Let's prayerfully apply these ideas as God leads and use the 5 Conversation Categories as a guideline to raise self-awareness of emotional bonds formed in conversation. This will help us guard our hearts just as Proverbs 4:23 encourages. As we do this, we can glorify God through healthy and satisfying relationships.

Stop and Discuss

1. What ideas in this booklet were new to you? What did you learn?

2. How can we encourage one another in emotional purity?

3. List five of your friends, both same and opposite gender. Now think through the 5 Conversation Categories and how deep emotionally you have gone with each of your friends. Write that down next to each name. Now pray about them and ask God whether you should be pursuing deeper intimacy or backing off a bit with each person.

AUTHOR'S NOTE

I wrote this booklet after teaching this material to college students for over a decade. This is information I wish I had known when I was in my teens and early twenties. It would have helped me avoid a lot of heartache, both my own and others' that I naively caused. I hope it is a blessing and encouragement to you as you enjoy relationships and glorify God through them.

I could not have written this booklet without the help and support of my wonderful husband, Jeff. He sacrificed time and time again to free me up so I could write. I want to thank him and countless others who have reviewed, edited, and offered suggestions to make this book what it is today.

Special thanks to my former writing group: Deb Entsminger, Sue Tell, Jamie Clark, and the supportive staff at NavPress. And Kathleen Selje for helping me fine-tune that tricky definition! Thank you!

ABOUT THE AUTHOR

Sherry and her husband, Jeff, enjoy teaching about healthy conversations and emotional purity around the country. She loves helping others discover how to better "get" one another and enjoy deep and thriving relationships. To contact her, please e-mail emotionalintegrity@gmail.com, or connect with her on Facebook at https://www.facebook.com /Sherry-Graf-Author-745910648804001.

NOTES

PART I: THE HEART OF HEALTHY CONVERSATIONS
1. Paula Rinehart, *Sex and the Soul of a Woman: How God Restores the Beauty of Relationships from the Pain of Regret* (Grand Rapids, MI: Zondervan, 2010), 179–180.
2. Lysa Terkeurst, *The Best Yes: Making Wise Decision in the Midst of Endless Demands* (Nashville: Nelson, 2014), 188.

PART II: HOW TO HAVE HEALTHY CONVERSATIONS
1. Adapted from a workshop led by Tom Yeakley.
2. *Merriam-Webster's Collegiate Dictionary*, 11th ed., s.v. "defraud."

PART IV: EMOTIONAL PURITY AND DATING
1. Rinehart, *Sex and the Soul of a Woman*, 179.

PART V: EMOTIONAL PURITY AND MARRIAGE
1. Rinehart, *Sex and the Soul of a Woman*, 180.
2. Shirley P. Glass, "Infidelity," American Association for Marriage and Family Therapy, http://www.aamft .org/iMIS15/AAMFT/Content/consumer_updates /infidelity.aspx. Accessed October 26, 2015.

3. Monika Lewis, "The Truth about Emotional Affairs," Focus on the Family, 2006, http://www.focusonthefamily .com/marriage/divorce_and_infidelity/affairs_and_ adultery/truth_about_emotional_affairs.aspx#footnote1. Accessed April 14, 2014.
4. Paul E. Miller, *A Loving Life: In a World of Broken Relationships* (Wheaton: Crossway, 2014), 58.